1949 U.K.

YEARBOOK

ISBN: 9781790334933

This book gives a fascinating and informative insight into life in the United Kingdom in 1949. It includes everything from the most popular music of the year to the cost of a buying a new house. Additionally there are chapters covering people in high office, the best-selling films of the year and all the main news and events. Want to know which team won the FA Cup or which British personalities were born in 1949? All this and much more awaits you within.

INDEX

FIRST EDITION

1949

January
M	T	W	T	F	S	S
					1	2
3	4	5	6	7	8	9
10	11	12	13	14	15	16
17	18	19	20	21	22	23
24	25	26	27	28	29	30
31						

◑:7 ○:14 ◐:21 ●:29

February
M	T	W	T	F	S	S
	1	2	3	4	5	6
7	8	9	10	11	12	13
14	15	16	17	18	19	20
21	22	23	24	25	26	27
28						

◑:6 ○:13 ◐:20 ●:27

March
M	T	W	T	F	S	S
	1	2	3	4	5	6
7	8	9	10	11	12	13
14	15	16	17	18	19	20
21	22	23	24	25	26	27
28	29	30	31			

◑:8 ○:14 ◐:21 ●:29

April
M	T	W	T	F	S	S
				1	2	3
4	5	6	7	8	9	10
11	12	13	14	15	16	17
18	19	20	21	22	23	24
25	26	27	28	29	30	

◑:6 ○:13 ◐:20 ●:28

May
M	T	W	T	F	S	S
						1
2	3	4	5	6	7	8
9	10	11	12	13	14	15
16	17	18	19	20	21	22
23	24	25	26	27	28	29
30	31					

◑:5 ○:12 ◐:19 ●:27

June
M	T	W	T	F	S	S
		1	2	3	4	5
6	7	8	9	10	11	12
13	14	15	16	17	18	19
20	21	22	23	24	25	26
27	28	29	30			

◑:4 ○:10 ◐:18 ●:26

July
M	T	W	T	F	S	S
				1	2	3
4	5	6	7	8	9	10
11	12	13	14	15	16	17
18	19	20	21	22	23	24
25	26	27	28	29	30	31

◑:3 ○:10 ◐:18 ●:25

August
M	T	W	T	F	S	S
1	2	3	4	5	6	7
8	9	10	11	12	13	14
15	16	17	18	19	20	21
22	23	24	25	26	27	28
29	30	31				

◑:1 ○:8 ◐:16 ●:24 ◑:30

September
M	T	W	T	F	S	S
			1	2	3	4
5	6	7	8	9	10	11
12	13	14	15	16	17	18
19	20	21	22	23	24	25
26	27	28	29	30		

○:7 ◐:15 ●:22 ◑:29

October
M	T	W	T	F	S	S
					1	2
3	4	5	6	7	8	9
10	11	12	13	14	15	16
17	18	19	20	21	22	23
24	25	26	27	28	29	30
31						

○:7 ◐:15 ●:21 ◑:28

November
M	T	W	T	F	S	S
	1	2	3	4	5	6
7	8	9	10	11	12	13
14	15	16	17	18	19	20
21	22	23	24	25	26	27
28	29	30				

○:5 ◐:13 ●:20 ◑:27

December
M	T	W	T	F	S	S
			1	2	3	4
5	6	7	8	9	10	11
12	13	14	15	16	17	18
19	20	21	22	23	24	25
26	27	28	29	30	31	

○:5 ◐:13 ●:19 ◑:27

PEOPLE IN HIGH OFFICE

Monarch - King George VI
Reign: 11th December 1936 - 6th February 1952
Predecessor: Edward VIII
Successor: Elizabeth II

Prime Minister

Clement Attlee
Labour Party
26th July 1945 - 26th October 1951

Australia

Canada

United States

Prime Minister
Ben Chifley
Labor Party
13th July 1945
- 19th December 1949

Prime Minister
Louis St. Laurent
Liberal Party
15th November 1948
- 21st June 1957

President
Harry S. Truman
Democratic Party
12th April 1945
- 20th January 1953

Brazil

President
Eurico Gaspar Dutra (1946-1951)

China

Premier
Sun Fo (1948-1949)
He Yingqin (1949)
Yan Xishan (1949-1950)

Cuba

President
Carlos Prío Socarrás (1948-1952)

France

President
Vincent Auriol (1947-1954)

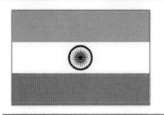

India

Prime Minister
Jawaharlal Nehru (1947-1964)

Ireland

Taoiseach of Ireland
John A. Costello (1948-1951)

Italy

Prime Minister
Alcide De Gasperi (1945-1953)

Japan

Prime Minister
Shigeru Yoshida (1948-1954)

Mexico

President
Miguel Alemán Valdés (1946-1952)

New Zealand

Prime Minister
Peter Fraser (1940-1949)
Sidney Holland (1949-1957)

Pakistan

Prime Minister
Liaquat Ali Khan (1947-1951)

Spain

President
Francisco Franco (1938-1973)

South Africa

Prime Minister
Daniel François Malan (1948-1954)

Soviet Union

Communist Party Leader
Joseph Stalin (1922-1953)

Turkey

Prime Minister
Hasan Saka (1947-1949)
Şemsettin Günaltay (1949-1950)

West Germany

Chancellor
Konrad Adenauer (1949-1963)

BRITISH NEWS & EVENTS

JAN

Mass Observation carries out a national survey, dubbed 'Little Kinsey', into the sexual behaviour and attitudes of 4,000 British men and women. Many of the findings were so outrageous they were suppressed and the survey remained largely unpublished for over fifty years.

1st   Peacetime conscription in the United Kingdom is regularised under the National Service Act 1948. Men aged 17-21 in England, Scotland and Wales are obliged to serve full-time in the armed forces for 18 months.

1st   The British Nationality Act 1948 comes into effect creating the status of Citizen of the United Kingdom and Colonies. This supersedes the existing shared status of Commonwealth Citizen.

4th January - RMS Caronia of the Cunard Line departs Southampton for New York on her maiden voyage. Launched on the 30th October 1947 by HRH The Princess Elizabeth and completed in December 1948, she served with Cunard until 1967. She was nicknamed the Green Goddess and is credited as one of the first dual-purpose built ships: suited to cruising, but also capable of transatlantic crossings.

31st   BBC Radio 4's long running radio programme, Book At Bedtime, debuts on the BBC Light Programme. It began with the first instalment of a 15-part reading of the John Buchan novel, The Three Hostages, read by Arthur Bush.

FEB

1st   The Women's Auxiliary Air Force, which had been founded in 1939, is renamed as the Women's Royal Air Force.

| 28th | Margaret Roberts, the future Prime Minister Margaret Thatcher, is adopted as the Conservative candidate for Dartford. She would go on to unsuccessfully fight two elections in the constituency (in 1950 and 1951) but it isn't until being selected as the candidate for Finchley in April 1958 that she was eventually elected as an MP (at the 1959 General Election). |

MAR

15th March - Clothes rationing, which began on the 1st June 1941, comes to an end.

Clothes rationing had been brought about due to a shortage of materials to make clothes and people had been urged to 'Make-do and Mend'. Everyone was given a Clothing Book with coloured coupons in it and every item of clothing was given a value in coupons. Each person was initially given 60 coupons to last them a year but this was later reduced to 48 coupons - children were allocated an extra 10 clothing coupons above the standard ration to allow for growing out of clothes. The coupon system allowed people to buy one completely new set of clothes a year.

| 24th | Laurence Olivier's film Hamlet (1948) becomes the first British film to win the Best Picture Oscar at the 21st Academy Awards in Hollywood, California. |
| 28th | Astronomer Fred Hoyle coins the term 'Big Bang' during a BBC Third Programme radio broadcast. |

APR

1st	The Marquess of Bath opens Longleat House to paying visitors and becomes the first stately home in Britain to be opened to the public on a commercial basis.
1st	The gas industry is nationalised in the United Kingdom. 1,062 privately owned and municipal gas companies are merged into twelve area gas boards, each a separate body with its own management structure.
4th	Britain and 11 other nations establish the North Atlantic Treaty Organization (NATO), a mutual defence pact aimed at containing possible Soviet aggression against Western Europe.
18th	Ireland formally becomes a republic and leaves the British Commonwealth.

20th	The first Badminton Horse Trials are held by the 10th Duke of Beaufort at Badminton House in Gloucestershire. The event had 22 horses from Britain and Ireland start, and was won by Golden Willow.
20th	Royal Navy frigate HMS Amethyst, on her way from Shanghai to Nanking to replace HMS Consort which was standing as guard ship for the British Embassy, comes under heavy fire from the Chinese People's Liberation Army (PLA) and runs aground off Rose Island.
24th	The wartime rationing of sweets and chocolate ends, but is re-instituted four months later as shortages return. The rationing of sweets eventually finishes for good on the 5th February 1953 when amongst the most popular sweets you could get in your local sweet shop were; lemon sherbets, flying saucers, barley sugar twists, liquorice allsorts, jelly babies, gobstoppers, Fry's chocolate creams, pear drops and cola cubes.
24th	Rose Heilbron and Helena Normanton become the first two women to be appointed King's Counsel in England.

24th April - The Manchester Mark 1 computer becomes operational at the Victoria University of Manchester. It is one of the earliest stored-program computers and its successful operation was widely reported in the British press, who used the phrase 'electronic brain' in describing it to their readers.

26th	The Ealing comedy film Passport To Pimlico premiers in London. It is the first of four comedies to be released by Ealing Studios during 1949, the others are; Whisky Galore, Kind Hearts And Coronets, and A Run For Your Money.
28th	The Commonwealth Prime Ministers' Conference issues the London Declaration, enabling India (and, thereafter, any other nation) to remain in the Commonwealth despite becoming a republic. It also created the position of Head of the Commonwealth (held by the ruling British monarch) and renamed the organisation from British Commonwealth to Commonwealth of Nations.
29th	The News Review reveals that neither the English public school Selhurst College nor its headmaster H. Rochester Sneath exists. These were in fact part of a practical joke in which student Humphry Berkeley impersonated H. Rochester Sneath, the headmaster of the rather odd Selhurst College, and wrote hoax letters to public figures.
30th	Wolverhampton Wanderers win the FA Cup for the first time in 41 years (and the third time in their history) with a 3-1 defeat of Leicester City at Wembley Stadium.

MAY

	The Council for Wales and Monmouthshire, set up to advise the government on matters of Welsh interest, has its first meeting.

MAY

13th	The English Electric Canberra, a first-generation jet-powered medium bomber, makes its first test flight piloted by Roland Beamont CBE, DSO & Bar, DFC & Bar.
10th	The first self-service launderette opens in Queensway, London.
29th	The first British Film Academy Awards take place at the Odeon Cinema, Leicester Square, in London, for films shown in the United Kingdom in 1947 and 1948. Chaired by British film producer Michael Balcon, the Academy bestowed accolades in three categories: Best British Film, Best Picture from any source, and a Special Award. The winners were Odd Man Out (1947), The Best Years of Our Lives (1946), and the Special Award went to the British documentary The World Is Rich (1947).

JUN

8th	George Orwell's dystopian novel Nineteen Eighty-Four is published in London by Secker & Warburg. Considered to be one of the most influential novels written during the twentieth century, the story focused on a futuristic totalitarian state that set out to control the thoughts of its citizens and rewrite history. The novel was an immediate success and was made into a movie in 1956 and 1984. The book was so influential that many of its made up terms have become part of normal speech, such as Big Brother, Thought Police and doublethink.

JUL

A BOAC Speedbird DeHavilland Comet shown in flight on the 25th January 1950.

27th July - The British-built DeHavilland Comet, the world's first commercial passenger jet airliner, makes its maiden flight at Hatfield in Hertfordshire. The Comet was created by De Havilland in Hertfordshire between 1947 and 1949. After that first test flight (which lasted for about thirty minutes) they continued to test the Comet and build prototypes until its commercial introduction in 1952. It was predicted to be a financial success but soon after its debut the Comet began suffering from several mechanical malfunctions, including incidents in which the jet broke up in mid-flight. After extensive research the problems were traced and the Comet redesigned. It remained in production in some form until the 1990's.

JUL

29th	The first regular weather forecasts begin on BBC television.
30th	The Legal Aid and Advice Act receives Royal Assent and establishes a much-extended system of legal aid in England and Wales. Similarly in Scotland the Legal Aid and Solicitors Act also receives Royal Assent.
31st	HMS Amethyst makes a break for freedom, after nightfall and under heavy fire, from the Chinese People's Liberation Army on both sides of the Yangtze River. The ship successfully rejoins the fleet at Woosung the next day.

AUG

22nd	T. S. Eliot's comedy, The Cocktail Party, premieres at the Edinburgh Festival. In 1950 the play went on to have successful runs in London and New York, with the Broadway production receiving the 1950 Tony Award for Best Play. The Cocktail Party was the most popular of Eliot's seven plays during his lifetime, but Murder In The Cathedral (1935) is probably the best remembered today.

Bomb damaged Old Trafford pictured shortly after the Second World War.

24th August - Old Trafford football stadium, home of Manchester United F.C., is re-opened following a comprehensive rebuild due to bomb damage by the Luftwaffe on the 11th March 1941. United's first game back saw them beat Bolton Wanderers 3-0 in front of 41,748 fans.

SEP

2nd	The film The Third Man, directed by Carol Reed, starring Joseph Cotten, Alida Valli and Orson Welles, is released in the United Kingdom. It would go on to win the Academy Award for Best Cinematography in 1950, and in 1999 the British Film Institute voted The Third Man the greatest British film of all time.
19th	The government devalue the pound by 30% against the U.S dollar (from $4.03 to $2.80). This major economic development subsequently caused 9 other countries to follow suit.

21st | Holyhead County School (Ysgol Uwchradd Caergybi) in Holyhead, Anglesey becomes the first comprehensive school to be opened in Wales.

30th September - The Berlin Airlift comes to an end after 15 months. The Airlift started as a result of the Berlin Blockade which was one of the first major international crises of the Cold War. During the multinational occupation of post–World War II Germany, the Soviet Union blocked the Western Allies' railway, road and canal access to the sectors of Berlin under Western control. In response, the Allies organised the Berlin Airlift to carry supplies to the people of West Berlin. Aircrews from the United States, Britain, Canada, Australia, New Zealand and South Africa flew over 200,000 flights in one year providing to the West Berliners up to 8,893 tons of necessities each day. By the spring of 1949 the airlift was clearly succeeding and by April it was delivering more cargo than had previously been transported into the city by rail. On the 12th May 1949 the USSR lifted the blockade of West Berlin but the Airlift continued until the 30th September to build up a comfortable surplus in the event of the Blockade restarting. By the end of the operation 17 American and 7 British planes had crashed delivering supplies to Soviet blockaded Berlin, and a total of 101 fatalities had been recorded (these were mostly due to non-flying accidents and included 40 Britons and 31 Americans).

OCT

	Valerie Hunter Gordon is granted a U.K. patent for what is considered to be the world's first disposable nappy, the PADDI. In 1950 Boots agreed to sell PADDI in all their branches and in 1951 the PADDI patent was granted for the U.S. and worldwide.
12th	John Boyd Orr wins the Nobel Peace Prize for his scientific research into nutrition and for his work as the first Director-General of the United Nations Food and Agriculture Organization (FAO).
26th	The first comedy series on British television, How Do You View?, starring Terry-Thomas, is broadcast on the BBC.

NOV

4th	Cwmbran is designated as the first New Town in Wales under the powers of the New Towns Act 1946. This Act, and later acts, were created in order to relocate populations in poor or bombed-out housing following the Second World War.
24th	The Iron And Steel Act is given Royal Assent and brings 94 iron and steel companies into public ownership.
28th	Winston Churchill makes a landmark speech in support of the idea of a European Union at Kingsway Hall, London.
29th	Ophthalmologist Sir Nicholas Harold Lloyd Ridley, a pioneer of intraocular lens surgery for cataract patients, achieves the first temporary implant of an intraocular lens at St Thomas' Hospital, London. Just a couple of months later, on the 8th February 1950, he would go on to implant a permanent artificial lens into an eye.

DEC

16th	The Parliament Act is given royal assent cutting the House of Lords veto to one year.
17th	Sutton Coldfield transmitting station becomes the first television transmitter to broadcast BBC Television to viewers outside London and the Home Counties. In terms of population covered today, it is the second most important transmitter in the U.K. after Crystal Palace in London.

The British ocean liner RMS Aquitania on her maiden voyage in New York Harbour (1914).

19th December - Cunard announce that the luxury passenger ship Aquitania would be withdrawn from service. On the 9th January 1950 Messrs Hampton & Sons Ltd were employed to auction the vessels furnishings and equipment, and later that month the ship was sold to the British Iron And Steel Corporation Ltd for £125,000. The ship then sailed from Southampton to Faslane in Scotland where she was broken up. The scrapping took almost a year to complete and ended an illustrious career which included steaming 3 million miles on 450 voyages. Aquitania had carried 1.2 million passengers over a career that spanned nearly 36 years, making her the longest-serving Express Liner of the 20th century and the only major liner to serve in both World Wars.

BRITISH PUBLICATIONS FIRST PRINTED IN 1949

- Enid Blyton's children's books, Little Noddy Goes To Toyland and The Secret Seven.
  - Agatha Christie's novel, Crooked House.
- H. F. Ellis' humorous collection, The Papers of A.J. Wentworth B.A.
  - Graham Greene's novella, The Third Man.
  - Nancy Mitford's novel, Love in a Cold Climate.
  - George Orwell's novel, Nineteen Eighty-Four.

NOTABLE BRITISH DEATHS

2nd Jan	John S. 'Jock' McNab (b. 17th April 1894) - Scottish international footballer who played predominantly for Liverpool during the period between the First and Second World Wars.
18th Apr	William Thomson Hay, FRAS (b. 6th December 1888) - Comedian, actor, author, film director and amateur astronomer. From 1934 to 1943 he was a prolific film star in Britain, and was ranked the third highest grossing star at the British Box Office in 1938 behind George Formby and Gracie Fields. Hay was also an amateur astronomer and in 1933 gained fame for discovering a Great White Spot on Saturn.
28th Apr	Sir Robert Robertson, KBE, FRS (b. 17th April 1869) - A chemist who served as HM Government's Government Chemist between 1921 and 1936, and the first person to establish that two types of natural diamond exist.
30th Aug	Arthur Fielder (b. 19th July 1877) - Professional cricketer and fast bowler who played for Kent County Cricket Club, and the England cricket team, between 1900 and 1914.
24th Oct	Thomas Rowland Hughes (b. 17th April 1903) - Welsh novelist, dramatist and poet who is primarily renowned in the present day for his novels about characters living and working in the slate quarries of northern Wales.
13th Dec	John Deans Hope (b. 8th May 1860) - Scottish Liberal politician.
16th Dec	George Maitland Lloyd Davies (b. 30th April 1880) - Welsh pacifist and MP for the University of Wales.

---

25 WORLDWIDE NEWS & EVENTS

1	6th January - The first photo of genes are taken with an electron microscope by assistant professor of anatomy Daniel C. Pease, and assistant professor of experimental medicine Richard F. Baker, at the University of Southern California in the United States.
2	10th January - RCA Victor introduce the first 45rpm, 7 inch record.
3	25th January - The first Emmy Awards are presented at the Hollywood Athletic Club in Los Angeles, California. The winners include Shirley Dinsdale, Pantomime Quiz (KTLA) and the made for television film, The Necklace.
4	25th January - David Ben-Gurion's Mapai party win the first Israeli legislative election with 35.7% of the vote.
5	24th February - A V-2/WAC-Corporal rocket becomes the first object to reach 5x the speed of sound (5,150mph) at White Sands Missile Range near Las Cruces in New Mexico.

6	2nd March - The world's first automatic street lights become operational in New Milford, Connecticut, U.S.
7	2nd March - The B-50 Superfortress Lucky Lady II lands in Fort Worth, Texas, after completing the first non-stop around-the-world airplane flight. It was refuelled in flight four times during the journey and was flown by Captain James Gallagher.
8	8th March - Australian Donald George Bradman plays his last innings in first class cricket, scoring 30. Often referred to as 'The Don', he is widely acknowledged as the greatest batsman of all time. Bradman's career Test batting average of 99.94 is often cited as the greatest achievement by any sportsman in any major sport.
9	4th May - An Italian Airlines Fiat G.212, carrying the entire Torino F.C. football team, crashes into the back wall of the Basilica of Superga killing all 31 people on board.
10	9th May - Prince Rainier III becomes monarch of Monaco. His coronation as 30th ruling Prince of Monaco takes place later in the year on the 19th November.
11	11th May - Siam renames itself Thailand.
12	11th May - Israel becomes 59th member of UN by a vote of 37-12.
13	11th June - Albert, a rhesus monkey, becomes the first primate astronaut after riding to a height of over 39 miles (63km) on board a U.S.-launched V-2 rocket. Albert unfortunately died of suffocation during the flight.
14	14th June - Albert II becomes the first primate in space in another U.S.-launched V-2 rocket. Albert II reached an altitude of 83 miles (134km) but again didn't fare so well dying on impact after a parachute failure. Astronauts Albert III and Albert IV were also launched on V-2 rockets later in 1949 but tragically Albert III died at 35,000ft in an explosion and Albert IV in another parachute failure.
15	8th July - South Africa's National Party begins implementing apartheid with the Prohibition of Mixed Marriages Act, prohibiting a white person to marrying a person of another race.
16	5th August - The Ambato earthquake in Ecuador, measuring 6.8 on the Richter scale, kills more than 5,000 people. The quake causes heavy damage to the city of Ambato and also destroys the nearby villages of Guano, Patate, Pelileo and Pillaro.
17	29th August - The USSR secretly performs its first nuclear test at the Semipalatinsk in Kazakhstan. Code named 'First Lightning' by the Soviets and 'Joe 1' by the Americans, the weapons' design was very similar to the American plutonium bomb that was dropped on Nagasaki, Japan, in 1945.
18	15th September - Konrad Adenauer is elected as the first Chancellor of the new created Federal Republic of Germany.
19	15th September - The hugely popular Lone Ranger premieres on the U.S. television channel ABC. The show would run for a total of 5 seasons and 221 episodes.
20	7th October - The German Democratic Republic is formed from the Soviet occupation zone in Germany. Four days later Wilhelm Pieck is elected its first President.
21	8th December - A typhoon strikes the Korean peninsula flattening hundreds of houses and reportedly killing 2,000 people.
22	1949 - Willard Libby and his colleagues at the University of Chicago discover a dating method that uses the naturally occurring radioisotope carbon-14 to determine the age of carbonaceous materials (radiocarbon dating). For his contributions to the team that developed this process, Libby was awarded the Nobel Prize in Chemistry in 1960.
23	1949 - American Gilmore Schjeldahl invents the airsickness bag.
24	1949 - Physicist Harold Lyons and his colleagues build the first atomic clock for the U.S. National Bureau of Standards. It was an ammonia maser device and although less accurate than existing quartz clocks it served to demonstrate the concept. The first accurate atomic clock, a caesium standard based on a certain transition of the caesium-133 atom, was built by Louis Essen and Jack Parry in 1955 at the National Physical Laboratory in the UK.
25	1949 - American Ed Seymour of Sycamore, Illinois invents aerosol spray paint.

U.K. PERSONALITIES

BORN IN 1949

Robert Allen Palmer
19th January 1949 -
26th September 2003

Singer-songwriter, musician and record producer known for his distinctive soulful voice. His first major break came with the band The Alan Bown Set in 1969 after he was invited to London to sing on their single Gypsy Girl. Palmer found success both in his solo career and with supergroup The Power Station. He received a number of awards throughout his career including two Grammy's for Best Male Rock Vocal Performance, an MTV Video Music Award, and two Brit Award nominations for Best British Male.

**Duncan Walker
Bannatyne**, OBE
2nd February 1949

Scottish entrepreneur, philanthropist and author whose business interests include hotels, health clubs, spas, media, TV, stage schools, property and transport. Bannatyne is probably best known for his appearances as one of the dragons on the BBC programme Dragons' Den (2005-2015) during which time he made investments in 36 businesses. He was appointed an OBE for his contribution to charity and is heavily involved with Comic Relief and UNICEF.

Lyn Paul
16th February 1949

Pop singer and actress born Lynda Susan Belcher. Paul came to fame as a member of the international chart-topping pop group The New Seekers in the early 1970s. She was the featured vocalist on their second placed 1972 Eurovision Song Contest entry, Beg, Steal or Borrow, and also lead vocalist on the 1973 No.1 hit You Won't Find Another Fool Like Me. Paul has more recently found success and critical acclaim starring in the long-running West End musical, Blood Brothers.

John Peter Rhys Williams, MBE, FRCS
2nd March 1949

Former rugby union footballer who represented Wales in international rugby during their Golden Era in the 1970s. He became known universally as J.P.R. Williams after 1973 when J.J. Williams joined the Welsh team. He is one of a small group of Welsh players to have won three Grand Slams and was one of the inaugural inductees of the International Rugby Hall of Fame in 1997. An orthopaedic surgeon by profession, he has continued to be involved in rugby since retirement and is currently serving as President of the Bridgend Ravens.

Martin McLean Buchan
6th March 1949

Former international footballer who played as a centre back for Aberdeen, Manchester United and Oldham Athletic. When he was signed by Manchester United's manager Frank O'Farrell in February 1972 for £120,000 he was the club's record signing. In total Buchan played in 34 international matches for Scotland between 1971 and 1978, including at the 1974 and 1978 World Cup Finals. He also captained Scotland twice: in 1975 against Romania and in 1977 against Argentina.

Kevin Reardon Lloyd
28th March 1949 -
2nd May 1998

Actor, best known for portraying DC Alfred 'Tosh' Lines in Thames Television's The Bill. Lloyd was one of the most popular members of The Bill and when it won the award for Best TV Drama at the National Television Awards (1996), it was Lloyd who collected it on behalf of the cast and crew. Prior to appearing in The Bill he had already had a part in Coronation Street and made a number of appearances in other shows such as Minder, Dempsey and Makepeace, Z-Cars, Auf Wiedersehen Pet, Blake's 7 and Casualty.

Alan Titchmarsh, MBE, DL, HonFSE
2nd May 1949

Gardener, presenter, and novelist who established himself as a media personality through appearances on Nationwide, coverage of the Chelsea Flower Show, Pebble Mill, and gardening programmes such as Gardener's World and Ground Force. Away from gardening he has had spells presenting Songs of Praise as well as a BBC nature documentary series, British Isles - A Natural History. Titchmarsh is also trustee of his own charity, Gardens for Schools, and other charities such as Seeds for Africa.

Zoë Wanamaker, CBE
13th May 1949

British actress of Canadian and American descent who has worked extensively with the Royal Shakespeare Company and the National Theatre. Her film appearances include Harry Potter and the Philosopher's Stone (2001), and My Week with Marilyn (2011), while her television roles have included starring as Tessa Piggott in Love Hurts (1992-1994) and Susan Harper in the long-running sitcom My Family (2000-2011). Wanamaker is a nine-time Olivier Award nominee, winning twice, and has also received four Tony Award nominations.

Richard Christopher 'Rick' Wakeman
18th May 1949

Keyboardist, songwriter, television and radio presenter, and author. He is best known for being part the progressive rock band Yes and for his solo albums released in the 1970s. He has made many television and radio appearances in recent years and has become known for his contributions to the BBC comedy series Grumpy Old Men, Watchdog and his radio show on Planet Rock (2005-2010). Wakeman has also written three books and in 2017 was inducted into the Rock and Roll Hall of Fame as a member of Yes.

James Broadbent
24th May 1949

Actor who graduated from the London Academy of Music and Dramatic Art in 1972. Broadbent has starred in numerous films achieving particular success in 2001 with three of the year's most popular films; Bridget Jones's Diary, Moulin Rouge!, for which he won a BAFTA, and Iris, for which he won an Oscar for his portrayal of John Bayley. In addition, for his television work, he won a British Academy Television Award and Golden Globe Award for Best Actor for his role as Lord Longford in the C4 drama Longford (2006).

Jeremy Bernard Corbyn
26th May 1949

Politician who has served as Leader of the Labour Party and Leader of the Opposition since 2015. He announced his candidacy for the Labour leadership following Labour's defeat in the 2015 general election. Despite only securing 35 nominations from fellow Labour MPs he quickly emerged as the leading candidate and was duly elected leader. In June 2016 Labour MPs passed a vote of no confidence in Corbyn but in the subsequent leadership contest he retained his position with an increased share of the vote.

Trevor Charles Horn,
CBE
15th July 1949

Music producer, songwriter, musician and singer. His influence on 1980s popular music was such that he has been called 'The Man Who Invented the Eighties'. Horn has produced commercially successful songs and albums for numerous British and international artists. As a musician he has had chart success with the bands The Buggles, Yes and Art of Noise. In 2010 he received the British Academy's Ivor Novello Award for Outstanding Contribution to British Music.

Roger Meddows Taylor
26th July 1949

Musician, singer and songwriter, best known as the drummer of the rock band Queen. Taylor was recognised early in his career for his unique sound and has been acclaimed as one of the most influential rock drummers of the 1970s and 1980s. As a member of Queen he is one of the world's best-selling music artists. In 1990 Queen received the Outstanding Contribution to British Music Award from the British Phonographic Industry and were inducted into the Rock and Roll Hall of Fame in 2001.

Mark Freuder Knopfler, OBE
12th August 1949

Singer-songwriter, guitarist, record producer, and film score composer. He is best known for having been the lead guitarist, lead singer and songwriter for the rock band Dire Straits, which he co-founded with his younger brother David in 1977. Dire Straits achieved worldwide success and sold in excess of 120 million records. Knopfler is a four-time Grammy Award winner and recipient of the Edison Award, the Steiger Award and the Ivor Novello Award. Since Dire Straits disbanded in 1995, Knopfler has recorded and produced eight solo albums.

John Anthony Curry,
OBE
9th September 1949 -
15th April 1994

Figure skater who won gold medals at both the Winter Olympics and World Championships in 1976. He was the flag bearer for Great Britain at the Winter Olympics and was later voted BBC Sports Personality of the Year. Along with Canadian skater Toller Cranston, Curry was responsible for bringing the artistic and presentation aspects of men's figure skating to a new level. Following his 1976 gold medal achievements Curry turned professional and founded a touring skating company.

Marjorie 'Mo' Mowlam
18th September 1949 -
19th August 2005

English Labour Party politician who was the Member of Parliament for Redcar from 1987 to 2001. During her time in office she served in the Cabinet as Secretary of State for Northern Ireland, Minister for the Cabinet Office and Chancellor of the Duchy of Lancaster (Mowlam's time as Northern Ireland Secretary saw the signing of the historic Good Friday Peace Agreement in 1998). Her personal charisma, and reputation for plain speaking, made her one of the most popular of New Labour's politicians.

Peter Leslie Shilton,
OBE
18th September 1949

Former footballer who played as a goalkeeper at 11 different clubs during a 30-year career. He currently holds the record for playing more games for England than anyone else, earning 125 caps, and holds the all-time record for the most competitive appearances in world football with 1,390. Internationally Shilton represented England at UEFA Euro 1980, the 1982 FIFA World Cup, the 1986 FIFA World Cup, UEFA Euro 1988 and the 1990 FIFA World Cup.

Lesley Lawson (née Hornby)
19th September 1949

Model, actress, and singer widely known by the nickname Twiggy. She was a British cultural icon and a prominent teenage model in swinging sixties London. In 1966 she was named The Face of 1966 by the Daily Express and voted British Woman of the Year. By 1967 she had modelled in France, Japan and the U.S., and had appeared on the covers of Vogue and The Tatler. After modelling Twiggy enjoyed a successful career as an actress and her role in The Boy Friend (1971) brought her two Golden Globe Awards.

Gerald Irving Ratner
1st November 1949

Businessman and motivational speaker who was formerly chief executive of the major British jewellery company Ratners Group (now the Signet Group). He achieved notoriety after making a speech in which he jokingly denigrated two of Ratners company's products which caused the company's value to plummet by around £500 million and very nearly resulted in the firm's collapse. Ratner now runs an export manufacturing company based India and the online jewellery business Gerald Online.

Nigel Allan Havers
6th November 1951

Actor who is probably best known for playing Lord Andrew Lindsay in the British film Chariots of Fire (1981) and Tom Latimer in the British TV comedy series Don't Wait Up (1983-1990). Despite appearing in such films as A Passage to India (1984), Empire of the Sun (1987) and Farewell to the King (1989), he never became a film star, but has continued in a succession of starring roles on television. Havers was the subject of This Is Your Life in 1992 when he was surprised by Michael Aspel.

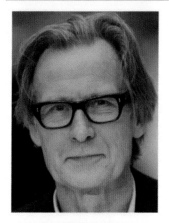

William Francis Nighy
12th December 1949

Actor and voice artist who worked in theatre and television before his first cinema role in Eye of the Needle (1981). Nighy made his name in television with The Men's Room (1991) in which he played the womaniser Prof. Mark Carleton, and became widely known for his performance as Billy Mack in Love Actually (2003). Other notable roles in cinema include his portrayal of Davy Jones in Pirates of the Caribbean film series, as well as Viktor in the Underworld film series.

Robert Lindsay Stevenson
13th December 1949

Stage and television actor known for his work with the Royal Shakespeare Company and in musical theatre, and for his roles as Wolfie Smith in Citizen Smith (1977-1980), Captain Pellew in Hornblower (1998-2003), and Ben Harper in My Family (2000-2011). During his career has he has won a BAFTA, a Tony Award, and three Olivier Awards for his work. On the 1st October 2016 he was given the Freedom of the Borough of Erewash in Derbyshire.

Paul Bernard Rodgers
17th December 1949

Singer, songwriter and musician best known for his success in the 1960s and 1970s as vocalist of Free and Bad Company. After stints in two less successful bands in the 1980s and early 1990s, The Firm and The Law, he became a solo artist. Rodgers has more recently toured and recorded with Queen. In 2011 he received the British Academy's Ivor Novello Award for Outstanding Contribution to British Music and a poll in Rolling Stone magazine ranked him number 55 on its list of the 100 Greatest Singers of All Time.

POPULAR MUSIC

Vaughn Monroe	No.1	Ghost Riders In The Sky
The Ink Spots	No.2	You're Breakin' My Heart
Burl Ives	No.3	Lavender Blue
Margaret Whiting	No.4	Far Away Places
Anne Shelton	No.5	The Wedding Of Lili Marlene
Gordon Jenkins & The Stardusters	No.6	I Don't See Me In Your Eyes Anymore
Perry Como (with The Fontane Sisters)	No.7	'A' You're Adorable
Vera Lynn	No.8	Again
Guy Lombardo & His Royal Canadians	No.9	Red Roses For A Blue Lady
Gracie Fields	No.10	For Ever And Ever

N.B. During this era music was dominated by a number of 'Big Bands' and songs could be attributed to the band leader, the band name, the lead singer or a combination of these. On top of this the success of a song was tied to the sales of sheet music, so a popular song would often be perfomed by many different combinations of singers and bands, and the contemporary charts would list the song without clarifying whose version was the major hit. With this in mind it should be noted that although the above chart has been compiled with best intent it remains subjective.

Vaughn Monroe
Ghost Riders In The Sky

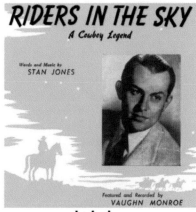

Label:	**Written by:**	**Length:**
His Master's Voice	Stan Jones	2 mins 56 secs

Vaughn Wilton Monroe (b. 7th October 1911 - d. 21st May 1973) was a baritone singer, trumpeter, big band leader and actor whose popularity was at its height in the 1940s and 1950s. Monroe formed his first orchestra in Boston in 1940 and became its principal vocalist. He has two stars on the Hollywood Walk of Fame one for recording and one for radio.

The Ink Spots
You're Breakin' My Heart

Label:	**Written by:**	**Length:**
Brunswick	Genaro / Skylar	3 mins 20 secs

The Ink Spots, Bill Kenny (b. 12th June 1914 - d. 23rd March 1978), Deek Watson (b. 18th July 1909 - d. 4th November 1969), Charlie Fuqua (b. 20th October 1910 - d. 21st December 1971), and Hoppy Jones (b. 17th February 1905 - d. 18th October 1944), were a pop vocal group who gained international fame in the 1930s and 1940s. In 1989 the Ink Spots were inducted into the Rock and Roll Hall of Fame, and in 1999 they were inducted into the Vocal Group Hall of Fame.

3 Burl Ives
Lavender Blue

Label:	**Written by:**	**Length:**
Decca	Eliot Daniel / Larry Morey	2 mins 19 secs

Burl Icle Ivanhoe Ives (b. 14th June 1909 - d. 14th April 1995) was an American singer and actor of stage, screen, radio and television. This version of Lavender Blue (Dilly, Dilly) was featured in the 1949 Walt Disney film So Dear To My Heart, and was nominated for Academy Award for Best Original Song (it lost to 'Baby, It's Cold Outside' from the film Neptune's Daughter). Other artists who also recorded Lavender Blue in 1949 included Vera Lynn, Sammy Kaye and Dinah Shore.

---

4 Margaret Whiting
Far Away Places

Label:	**Written by:**	**Length:**
Capitol Records	Kramer / Whitney	3 mins 16 secs

Margaret Eleanor Whiting (b. 22nd July 1924 - d. 10th January 2011) was a singer of popular and country music, whose career was at its peak during the 1940s and 1950s. Whiting's first recordings were as featured singer with various orchestras. In 1945 she began to record under her own name and had a number of hits including; A Tree In The Meadow, Far Away Places, and Slippin' Around.

Anne Shelton
The Wedding Of Lili Marlene

Label:	**Written by:**	**Length:**
Decca	Reine / Connor	2 mins 31 secs

Anne Shelton, OBE (b. 10th November 1923 - d. 31st July 1994) was a popular English vocalist who is best remembered for providing inspirational songs for soldiers both on radio broadcasts, and in person, at British military bases during the Second World War. In 1990 Shelton was awarded the OBE for her work with the Not Forgotten Association, a charitable organisation for disabled former service personnel from all wars.

Gordon Jenkins & The Stardusters
I Don't See Me In Your Eyes Anymore

Label:	**Written by:**	**Length:**
Decca	Benjamin / Weiss	3 mins 10 secs

Gordon Hill Jenkins (b. 12th May 1910 - d. 1st May 1984) was an American arranger, composer and pianist who was an influential figure in popular music in the 1940s and 1950s. Early in 1949 Jenkins teamed up with the **Stardusters** (pictured above circa 1940, with Glen Galyon, Curt Purnell, Dick Wylder, and May McKim) to land this popular hit recording, I Don't See Me In Your Eyes Anymore.

7 Perry Como (with The Fontane Sisters)
'A' You're Adorable

Label:	**Written by:**	**Length:**
His Master's Voice	Kaye / Wise / Lippman	2 mins 23 secs

Pierino Ronald 'Perry' Como (b. 18th May 1912 - d. 12th May 2001) was a singer and television personality. During a career spanning more than half a century he recorded exclusively for RCA Victor, sold millions of records and pioneered a weekly musical variety television show which proved to be one of the most successful in television history. **The Fontane Sisters** were a trio consisting of Bea, Geri and Marge Rosse who appeared on several recordings backing up Como.

---

8 Vera Lynn
Again

Label:	**Written by:**	**Length:**
London Records	Cochran / Newman	3 mins 12 secs

Dame Vera Margaret Lynn, CH DBE OStJ (née Welch; b. 20th March 1917), widely known as 'the Forces' Sweetheart', is a singer, songwriter and actress, whose musical recordings and performances were enormously popular during World War 2. During the war she toured Egypt, India and Burma as part of ENSA, giving outdoor concerts for the troops. 'Again' first appeared in the movie Road House (1948), sung by Ida Lupino. By 1949 there were a number of recordings of this song including versions by Vic Damone, Doris Day, Tommy Dorsey, Gordon Jenkins, Art Mooney and of course Vera Lynn.

Guy Lombardo & His Royal Canadians
Red Roses For A Blue Lady

Label:	Written by:	Length:
Decca	Roy Brodsky / Sid Tepper	2 mins 45 secs

Gaetano Alberto 'Guy' Lombardo (b. 19th June 1902 - d. 5th November 1977) was a bandleader and violinist of Italian descent. Forming The Royal Canadians in 1924 with his brothers Carmen, Lebert and Victor, and other musicians from his hometown, Lombardo led the group to international success. They billed themselves as creating 'the sweetest music this side of Heaven'. The Lombardo's are believed to have sold between 100 and 300 million records during their lifetimes.

Gracie Fields
For Ever And Ever

Label:	Written by:	Length:
London Records	Franz Winkler	2 mins 52 secs

Dame Gracie Fields, DBE (b. Grace Stansfield; 9th January 1898 - d. 27th September 1979) was an actress, singer, comedian, and a star of both cinema and music hall. There were a number of popular recordings of the song 'For Ever And Ever' in 1949, including versions by Russ Morgan, Perry Como, Margaret Whiting and Dinah Shore. The songs English lyrics were written by Malia Rosa in 1948 to the music of the 1930 German song, 'Fliege mit mir in die Heimat' (written by the Austrian songwriter Franz Winkler).

1949: TOP FILMS

1. **Samson And Delilah** - *Paramount*
2. **Jolson Sings Again** - *Columbia*
3. **Sands Of Iwo Jima** - *Republic*
4. **Battleground** - *MGM*
5. **I Was A Male War Bride** - *20th Century Fox*

OSCARS

Best Picture: All The King's Men

Best Director: Joseph L. Mankiewicz *(A Letter To Three Wives)*

Best Actor:	**Best Actress:**
Broderick Crawford *(All The King's Men)*	Olivia de Havilland *(The Heiress)*
Best Supporting Actor:	**Best Supporting Actress:**
Dean Jagger *(Twelve O'Clock High)*	Mercedes McCambridge *(All The King's Men)*

SAMSON AND DELILAH

Directed by: Cecil B. DeMille - Runtime: 2 hours 11 minutes

The biblical story of strongman Samson and his love for Delilah, the woman who seduces him, discovers the secret of his strength, and then betrays him to the Philistines.

STARRING

Hedy Lamarr
Born: 9th November 1914
Died: 19th January 2000

Character:
Delilah

Austrian-born American film actress and inventor, born Hedwig Eva Maria Kiesler. After a brief film career in Czechoslovakia, which included the controversial film Ecstasy (1933), she met MGM studio head Louis B. Mayer in Paris whilst he was scouting for talent in Europe. He offered her a movie contract in Hollywood and she became a film star from the late 1930s to the 1950s. Lamarr's biggest success was with her portrayal of Delilah in Samson and Delilah.

Victor John Mature
Born: 29th January 1913
Died: 4th August 1999

Character:
Samson

American stage, film, and television actor who starred most notably in several Biblical movies during the 1950s, and was known for his dark good looks and mega-watt smile. His best known film roles include One Million B.C. (1940), My Darling Clementine (1946), Kiss Of Death (1947), Samson And Delilah, and The Robe (1953). He also appeared in a large number of musicals opposite such stars as Rita Hayworth and Betty Grable.

George Henry Sanders
Born: 3rd July 1906
Died: 25th April 1972

Character:
The Saran of Gaza

Russian-born English film and television actor, singer-songwriter, music composer, and author. His career as an actor spanned more than 40 years and he was often cast as sophisticated but villainous characters. He is perhaps best known for his roles as Jack Favell in Rebecca (1940), Addison DeWitt in All About Eve (1950), for which he won an Academy Award, and as Simon Templar, 'The Saint', in five films made in the 1930s and 1940s.

TRIVIA

Goofs | In the final destruction-of-the-temple scene, the huge statue of Dagon starts to topple head first, but in later shots it is seen sliding towards the camera feet first. This is because director Cecil DeMille was not satisfied with the first take and had the temple re-erected then collapsed a second time. Shots from both destructions were spliced together to make an exciting but rather puzzling final sequence.

Interesting Facts | Victor Mature won the role of Samson over Burt Lancaster. Lancaster was suffering from a back injury at the time and was ultimately considered too young for the part.

CONTINUED

Interesting Facts
With Samson And Delilah grossing $28 million domestically in the United States, it became Paramount's biggest hit since DeMille's silent version of The Ten Commandments (1923).

For the scene in which Samson kills the lion, Victor Mature refused to wrestle a tame movie lion. Told by director Cecil B. DeMille that the lion had no teeth, Mature replied, "I don't want to be gummed to death, either." The scene shows a stunt man wrestling the tame lion, intercut with close-ups of Mature wrestling a lion skin.

Much discussion took place during the shooting of the scene where Samson kisses Delilah as to whether a man kisses a woman with his eyes closed or open. Victor Mature insisted that a fellow would be a chump to close his eyes when kissing Hedy Lamarr. In the final shot, Mature closed, opened, and then closed his eyes again.

Of Samson And Delilah's five Academy Award nominations the film won two, for Best Art Direction and Best Costume Design.

At the premiere, Cecil B. DeMille asked Groucho Marx what he thought of the film. Groucho replied, "Well, there's just one problem, C.B. No picture can hold my interest where the leading man's tits are bigger than the leading lady's." DeMille was not amused, by Marx's remark, but Victor Mature apparently was.

Quotes
Prince Ahtur: This Samson has some unknown power, some secret that gives him superhuman strength. No man can stand against him.
Delilah: Perhaps he'll fall before a woman. Even Samson's strength must have a weakness. There isn't a man in the world who would not share his secrets with some woman.

Samson: You came to this house as wedding guests. Fire and death are your gifts to my bride. For all that I do against you now, I shall be blameless. I'll give you back fire for fire, and death for death!

Directed by: Henry Levin - Runtime: 1 hour 36 minutes

In this sequel to The Jolson Story (1946), we pick up the singer's career just as he has returned to the stage after a premature retirement.

STARRING

Larry Parks
Born: 13th December 1914
Died: 13th April 1975

Character:
Al Jolson / Larry Parks

Stage and movie actor born Samuel Klausman Lawrence Parks. His career arced from bit player and supporting roles to top billing, before his career was virtually ended when he admitted to having once been a member of a Communist party cell (this led to him being blacklisted by all Hollywood studios). His best known role was as Al Jolson, whom he portrayed in two films: The Jolson Story (1946) and Jolson Sings Again.

Barbara Hale
Born: 18th April 1922
Died: 26th January 2017

Character:
Ellen Clark

Actress best known for her role as legal secretary Della Street on more than 270 episodes of the Perry Mason television series (1957-1966), which earned her the 1959 Emmy Award for Outstanding Supporting Actress in a Drama Series. She reprised the role in 30 Perry Mason movies for television. Her most notable film roles include Higher And Higher (1943), West Of The Pecos (1945), Lady Luck (1946), The Window (1949) and Jolson Sings Again.

William Demarest
Born: 27th February 1892
Died: 27th December 1983

Character:
Steve Martin

Character actor popularly known for playing Uncle Charley in the American sitcom My Three Sons (1965-1972). A veteran of World War I, he became a prolific film and television actor. Demarest appeared in over 140 films throughout his career and received an Academy Award nomination during this time for his supporting role in The Jolson Story (1946). He had previously shared the screen with the real Al Jolson in The Jazz Singer (1927).

TRIVIA

Interesting Facts

After appearing as himself in a long shot of 'Swanee' (uncredited) in The Jolson Story (1946), Al Jolson had wanted to make an appearance as himself in this film too. Although he didn't actually get to play himself, he does appear. During the filming of 'The Jolson Story' the man standing watching the filming in a grey cowboy hat is Jolson.

The film was nominated for three Academy Awards: Cinematography (Colour), Music (Scoring of a Musical Picture) and Writing (Story and Screenplay).

CONTINUED

Interesting Facts	'Lux Radio Theater' broadcast a 60-minute radio adaptation of the movie on the 22nd May 1950, with Barbara Hale and William Demarest reprising their film roles. Al Jolson, who provides the singing for Larry Parks in the film, plays himself.

According to an interview with Ray Henderson, one of the composers of 'Sonny Boy', the song was written as a satire. They were tired of Al Jolson's Mammy-type songs and wanted to write one so syrupy and sentimental that he wouldn't sing it. He heard it, loved it, changed a few of the lyrics and made it his signature tune.

For the film Al Jolson auditioned to play himself.

In this sequel, the story reaches the point in Jolson's life where a film of his life is to be made (first film: The Jolson Story), and in preparation for the film Jolson meets the actor who is to portray him. In what is probably a cinema first, Parks plays both Jolson and himself (the young Larry Parks) as they meet in a split-screen scene. |
| **Quote** | **Ellen Clark**: *[leaving room]*
My! We'll soon be smart as pigs! |

SANDS OF IWO JIMA

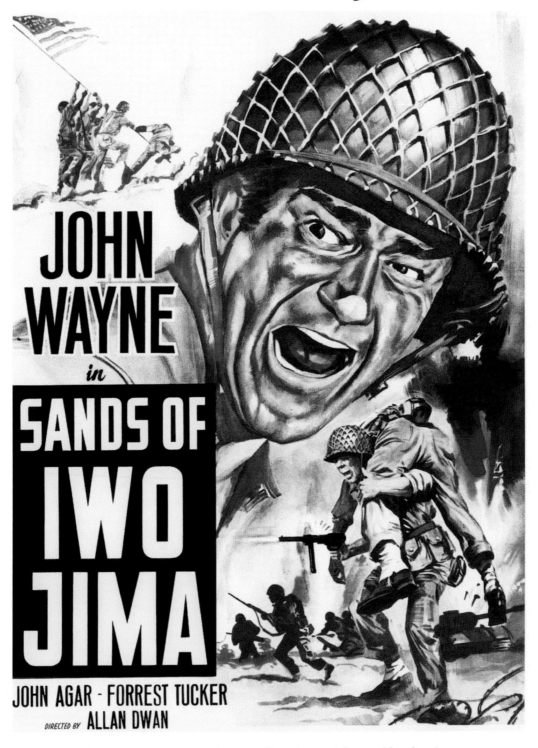

Directed by: Allan Dwan - Runtime: 1 hour 40 minutes

After his wife takes their son and leaves him, Sgt. John Stryker is an embittered man who takes his misery out a bunch of green recruits who have a hard time dealing with his tough drills and thick skin. In the end, as survival in the bloody battle of Iwo Jima depends on the lessons he has taught them, his troops discover why he was so tough.

STARRING

John Wayne
Born: 26th May 1907
Died: 11th June 1979

Character:
Sgt. John M. Stryker

Actor, director and producer who was born Marion Robert Morrison. Nicknamed Duke, his career took off in 1939 with John Ford's Stagecoach making him an instant star. Wayne went on to feature in a further 141 pictures and was nominated for an Academy Award on three occasions, winning once for Best Actor in True Grit (1969). He was posthumously awarded the Presidential Medal of Freedom on the 9th June 1980.

John George Agar, Jr.
Born: 31st January 1921
Died: 7th April 2002

Characters:
PFC Peter Conway

Actor best known for starring alongside John Wayne in the films Sands Of Iwo Jima, Fort Apache (1948), and She Wore A Yellow Ribbon (1949). In his later career he developed a niche playing leading men in low-budget science fiction, Western, and horror movies. He was the star of B movies such as Tarantula (1955), The Mole People (1956), and The Brain From Planet Arous (1957). Agar was married to Shirley Temple for 5 years until their divorce in 1950.

Adele Mara
Born: 28th April 1923
Died: 7th May 2010

Character:
Allison Bromley

Spanish-American actress, singer, and dancer born Adelaida Delgado. She started her career aged 15 as a singer/dancer with Xavier Cugat and His Orchestra in Detroit. Cugat took her to New York where she was spotted by a Columbia talent scout. Mara appeared in many films during the 1940s and 1950s, and was also a popular pinup girl. Her career continued on television in the 1950s and 1960s, and she featured in a number of guest roles, primarily in westerns.

TRIVIA

Goofs	In the training scenes, set in New Zealand, a row of Eucalyptus trees are seen. These are native to Australia and are not found in New Zealand.
	Near the beginning of the film, while the platoon is marching and Conway is talking about his Father, his helmet strap keeps switching from swinging lose to being tucked under his rifle strap.
Interesting Facts	Kirk Douglas was considered for the role of Sgt. Stryker before director Allan Dwan realised he could get John Wayne to play the part.

CONTINUED

Interesting Facts

This film recreates the famous 'Raising Of The Flag' photograph taken on Iwo Jima by Joe Rosenthal on the 23rd February, 1945. The three surviving flag raisers from that day make a cameo appearance during this scene. Rene A. Gagnon, Ira H. Hayes and John H. Bradley are seen with John Wayne as he instructs them to hoist the flag. The flag used to recreate the incident is the actual flag that was raised on Mount Suribachi and was loaned to the movie by the U.S. Marine Corps Museum.

At $1.4 million this was the most expensive movie Republic Pictures had ever made. It went on to gross $13.9 million.

Sands Of Iwo Jima gave John Wayne his first ever Academy Award nomination for Best Actor (won by Broderick Crawford in 'All The King's Men'). Wayne wouldn't be nominated again for 20 years until True Grit (1969), when he would win the Best Actor Award for playing Reuben J. 'Rooster' Cogburn.

Quotes

Sgt. Stryker: You gotta learn right and you gotta learn fast. And any man that doesn't want to cooperate, I'll make him wish he had never been born.

PFC. Al Thomas: I got a great future, for the next couple of hours.

BATTLEGROUND

Directed by: William A. Wellman - Runtime: 1 hour 58 minutes

A squad of the 101st Airborne Division copes with being trapped in the besieged city of Bastogne during the Battle of the Bulge.

STARRING

Van Johnson
Born: 25th August 1916
Died: 12th December 2008

Character:
Holley

Film/television actor and dancer who was a major star at Metro-Goldwyn-Mayer during and after World War II. Born Charles Van Dell it was his embodiment of the boy-next-door wholesomeness that made him a popular Hollywood star in the 1940s and 1950s. Johnson's big break was in A Guy Named Joe (1943), starring Spencer Tracy and Irene Dunne. In 1945, Johnson tied with Bing Crosby as the top box office star chosen by the National Association of Theatre Owners.

John Hodiak
Born: 16th April 1914
Died: 19th October 1955

Character:
Jarvess

American actor of Ukrainian and Polish descent who worked in radio, stage and film. Hodiak arrived in Hollywood in 1942 and signed a motion picture contract with MGM. Hodiak first came to notice in Alfred Hitchcock's classic Lifeboat (1944) and followed this with equally fine performances in A Bell For Adano (1945) and Somewhere In The Night (1946). Perhaps his best known credit was as Judy Garland's leading man in The Harvey Girls (1946).

Ricardo Montalban
Born: 25th November 1920
Died: 14th January 2009

Character:
Roderigues

Mexican actor (born Ricardo Gonzalo Pedro Montalbán y Merino) whose career spanned seven decades. Among his notable roles were Armando in the Planet Of The Apes film series and Khan Noonien Singh in the film Star Trek II: The Wrath of Khan (1982). His best-known television roles were that of Mr Roarke on the television series Fantasy Island (1977-1984), his Emmy Award winning role in How the West Was Won (1976) and as a villain in the The Colbys (1985-1987).

TRIVIA

Goofs	When Holley hears Denise and Jarvess talking on the other side of the living room door he rushes into the corridor with a full cup of coffee. He takes one small sip and then puts, what is now an empty cup, in to his pocket.
	When the C-47s are dropping supplies to the soldiers, one of the stock footage pieces used shows paratroopers jumping from planes, not supplies being dropped.
Interesting Facts	Twenty veterans of the 101st Airborne who fought in the Bastogne area were hired to train the actors and were also used as extras.

CONTINUED

Interesting Facts   James Whitmore took over the role of Sergeant Kinnie after James Mitchell was fired for moving too much like a dancer and not enough like a drill sergeant.

James Arness (Garby) served in World War II and is the most decorated of the actors in the film. He received the Bronze Star, the Purple Heart, the European-African-Middle Eastern Campaign Medal with three bronze campaign stars, the World War II Victory Medal, and the Combat Infantryman Badge for his service.

Douglas Fowley (Private Kippton - who continually loses his false teeth) served in the Navy in the South Pacific in World War II, and lost all of his own teeth in an explosion aboard his aircraft carrier during battle.

A private showing of the film for President Harry S. Truman was arranged (even before the premiere in Washington, D.C. on the 9th November 1949) which was attended by Brigadier General Anthony McAuliffe who had commanded the 101st during the siege.

Battleground was MGM's largest grossing film in five years and was nominated for 6 Academy Awards, winning two for; Best Writing, Story and Screenplay, and Best Cinematography, (Black-and-White).

Quote   *[as Bettis is digging a foxhole]*
Holley: Let's not try to reach China this time, hey Bettis?
Bettis: Well there's no sense digging if you don't go deep.
Holley: The last one we dug one together, you went so deep that when I climbed out in the morning I got the bends.

I WAS A MALE WAR BRIDE

Directed by: Howard Hawks - Runtime: 1 hour 45 minutes

After marrying American Lieutenant Catherine Gates, with whom he was assigned to work in post-war Germany, French Captain Henri Rochard tries to return to America under the auspices of America's 1945 War Brides Act.

STARRING

Cary Grant
Born: 18th January 1904
Died: 29th November 1986

Character:
Capt. Henri Rochard

British-American actor (born Archibald Alec Leach) who is best known as one of classic Hollywood's definitive leading men. He began a career in Hollywood in the early 1930s and became known for his transatlantic accent, light-hearted approach to acting, comic timing and debonair demeanour. He was twice nominated for the Academy Award for Best Actor for his roles in; Penny Serenade (1941) and None But The Lonely Heart (1944).

Clara Lou 'Ann' Sheridan
Born: 21st February 1915
Died: 21st January 1967

Character:
Lt. Catherine Gates

Actress and singer who made an uncredited film debut aged 19 in Search For Beauty (1934). She worked regularly from 1934 to her death in 1967, first in film and later in television. Notable film roles include Angels With Dirty Faces (1938), The Man Who Came To Dinner (1942), Kings Row (1942), Nora Prentiss (1947) and I Was A Male War Bride. In television she starred in the soap opera Another World (1964) and the Western series Pistols 'n' Petticoats (1966).

Marion Marshall
Born: 8th June 1929

Characters:
Lt. Kitty Lawrence

Retired actress born Marian Lepriel Tanner. Her first film appearances were in the 20th Century Fox films Gentleman's Agreement and Daisy Kenyon in 1947 (both uncredited). She went on to play roles (many minor) in over 25 more films until 1967. Marshall had a small but significant role in I Was A Male War Bride and featured prominently in three Dean Martin and Jerry Lewis comedy films, That's My Boy (1951) The Stooge (1952), and Sailor Beware (1952).

TRIVIA

Goofs	When Catherine and Henri come up to the dam, Henri is rowing. He jumps to the front of the boat to look over the edge. When he does so he drops the starboard oar into the water. The next scene shows him looking over the edge and when the camera cuts back to the aerial view you can see that both oars are now on the boat.
Interesting Facts	Eleanor Audley, whose voice was used to dub the assignment officer, was also the voice of some of Disney's greatest villains; Lady Tremaine the evil stepmother from Cinderella (1950), and the evil fairy, Maleficent, from Sleeping Beauty (1959).

CONTINUED

Interesting Facts
Howard Hawks was given license to cast whomever he wanted in the supporting roles, so he cast his current girlfriend, Marion Marshall, in the role of Lt. Kitty Lawrence.

This was Howard Hawks' first film to be shot in Europe and it was beset with problems. The German winter was unbearably cold and most of the cast and crew fell ill. Ann Sheridan caught pleurisy (which developed into pneumonia), Cary Grant contracted hepatitis with jaundice, and Hawks broke out in hives. Due to the various illnesses of cast members the delay in production pushed the films budget to over $2 million.

Quote
Soldier: You're not Mrs. Rochard!
Capt. Henri Rochard: I'm MISTER Rochard.
Soldier: Well, it's your WIFE who must report here for transportation to Bremerhaven.
Capt. Henri Rochard: According to the War Department, I AM my wife.
Soldier: You can't be your wife!
Capt. Henri Rochard: If the American army says that I CAN be my wife, who am I to dispute them?

Sporting Winners

Five Nations Rugby
Ireland

Position	Nation	Played	Won	Draw	Lost	For	Against	+/-	Points
1	**Ireland**	**4**	**3**	**0**	**1**	**41**	**24**	**+17**	**6**
2	England	4	2	0	2	35	29	+6	4
3	France	4	2	0	2	24	28	-4	4
4	Scotland	4	2	0	2	20	37	-17	4
5	Wales	4	1	0	3	17	19	-2	2

The 1949 Five Nations Championship was the twentieth series of the rugby union Five Nations Championship. Including the previous incarnations as the Home Nations and Five Nations, this was the fifty-fifth series of the northern hemisphere rugby union championship. Ten matches were played between the 15th January and 26th March, with Ireland winning its 6th title and the Triple Crown.

Date	Team		Score		Team	Location
15-01-1949	France		0-8		Scotland	Paris
15-01-1949	Wales		9-3		England	Cardiff
29-01-1949	Ireland		9-16		France	Dublin
05-02-1949	Scotland		6-5		Wales	Edinburgh
12-02-1949	Ireland		14-5		England	Dublin
26-02-1949	England		8-3		France	Twickenham
26-02-1949	Scotland		3-13		Ireland	Edinburgh
12-03-1949	Wales		0-5		Ireland	Swansea
19-03-1949	England		19-3		Scotland	Twickenham
26-03-1949	France		5-3		Wales	Paris

Calcutta Cup

England ✚ 19-3 ✖ Scotland

The Calcutta Cup was first awarded in 1879 and is the rugby union trophy awarded to the winner of the match (currently played as part of the Six Nations Championship) between England and Scotland. The Cup was presented to the Rugby Football Union after the Calcutta Football Club in India disbanded in 1878. It is made from melted down silver rupees withdrawn from the clubs funds.

BRITISH GRAND PRIX - TOULO DE GRAFFENRIED

Toulo de Graffenried in his race winning Maserati 4CLT at Silverstone.

The 1949 British Grand Prix was held at Silverstone on the 14th May. The race was won by Baron Emmanuel 'Toulo' de Graffenried (from 4th on the grid) driving a Maserati over 100 laps of the 2.89 mile circuit. The fastest lap of 2 minutes 10.4 seconds went to Prince Bira of Siam, also driving a Maserati.

Pos.	Country	Driver	Car
1	**Switzerland**	**Toulo de Graffenried**	**Maserati**
2	United Kingdom	Bob Gerard	ERA
3	France	Louis Rosier	Talbot-Lago

Silverstone first hosted the British Grand Prix in 1948 and is built on the site of the World War II Royal Air Force bomber station, RAF Silverstone. The airfield's three runways, in a classic WWII triangular format, lie within the outline of the present track.

1949 GRAND PRIX SEASON

Date	Grand Épreuves	Circuit	Winning Driver	Constructor
15th May	British Grand Prix	Silverstone	Toulo de Graffenried	Maserati
19th Jun	Belgian Grand Prix	Spa	Louis Rosier	Talbot-Lago-Talbot
3rd Jul	Swiss Grand Prix	Bremgarten	Alberto Ascari	Ferrari
17th Jul	French Grand Prix	Reims-Gueux	Louis Chiron	Talbot-Lago-Talbot
11th Sep	Italian Grand Prix	Monza	Alberto Ascari	Ferrari

The 1949 Grand Prix season was the fourth post-war year for Grand Prix racing and the final year before the beginning of the Formula One World Championship. There was no organised championship in 1949, although several of the more prestigious races were recognised as Grandes Epreuves (great trials) by the FIA. Alberto Ascari and Juan Manuel Fangio proved to be the most successful drivers, each winning five Grands Prix. Maserati's cars were the most successful brand winning 10 of the season's 27 Grand Prix races.

GRAND NATIONAL - RUSSIAN HERO

The 1949 Grand National was the 103rd renewal of this world famous horse race and took place at Aintree Racecourse near Liverpool on the 26th March. Russian Hero, trained by George Owen and ridden by jockey Leo McMorrow, won the race by eight lengths.

Fourty-three horses contested the 1949 National and competed for the £13,000 in prize money. Of the 43 runners only 11 horses completed the course; 26 fell, 4 were brought down, 1 refused and 1 was run out.

	Name	Jockey	Age	Weight	Odds
1st	**Russian Hero**	**Leo McMorrow**	**9**	**10st 8lb**	**66/1**
2nd	Roimond	Dick Francis	8	11st 12lb	22/1
3rd	Royal Mount	Patrick Doyle	10	10st 12lb	18/1
4th	Cromwell	Anthony Mildmay	8	11st 3lb	6/1
5th	Flaming Steel	Joe Spencer	8	10st 9lb	33/1

EPSOM DERBY - NIMBUS

The Derby Stakes is Britain's richest horse race and the most prestigious of the country's five Classics. First run in 1780 this Group 1 flat horse race is open to three year old thoroughbred colts and fillies. The race takes place at Epsom Downs in Surrey over a distance of one mile, four furlongs and 10 yards (2,423 metres) and is scheduled for early June each year.

Photo: British Thoroughbred racehorse Nimbus (1946-1972) is seen being led in by its owner Marion Glenister after winning the 1949 Epsom Derby. The result of the race was decided, for the very first time, by a photo-finish.

FOOTBALL LEAGUE CHAMPIONS

England

Pos.	Team	W	D	L	F	A	Pts.
1	**Portsmouth**	**25**	**8**	**9**	**84**	**42**	**58**
2	Manchester United	21	11	10	77	44	53
3	Derby County	22	9	11	74	55	53
4	Newcastle United	20	12	10	70	56	52
5	Arsenal	18	13	11	74	44	49

Scotland

Pos.	Team	W	D	L	F	A	Pts.
1	**Rangers**	**20**	**6**	**4**	**63**	**32**	**46**
2	Dundee	20	5	5	71	48	45
3	Hibernian	17	5	8	75	52	39
4	East Fife	16	3	11	64	46	35
5	Falkirk	12	8	10	70	54	32

FA CUP WINNERS - WOLVERHAMPTON WANDERERS

Leicester City   1-3   Wolverhampton Wanderers
Griffiths ⚽ 47'   Pye ⚽ 13' ⚽ 42' / Smyth ⚽ 64'

The 1949 FA Cup Final took place on the 30th April at Wembley Stadium in front of 98,920 fans. Wolves, boasting several England internationals among their ranks, beat second division Leicester City who making their first Wembley appearance. Wolves Captain Billy Wright was presented with the cup by HRH The Princess Elizabeth.

GOLF - OPEN CHAMPIONSHIP - BOBBY LOCKE

The 1949 Open Championship was the 78th to be played and was held between the 6th and 9th July at Royal St George's Golf Club in Sandwich, Kent. Bobby Locke of South Africa won the first of his four Open titles, in a 36-hole playoff with Harry Bradshaw of Ireland, to take the Claret Jug and winner's prize money of £300.

WORLD SNOOKER CHAMPIONSHIP - FRED DAVIS

Photos: 1. Fred Davis / 2. Fred Davis (far right) with his mother and brother Joe.

Fred Davis   80 - 65   Walter Donaldson

The 1949 World Snooker Championship was held at the Leicester Square Hall in London between the 21st February and 7th May. Davis won his second World title by defeating Donaldson 80-65 in the final, and became only the second player to defend his first world title after brother Joe Davis in 1928. Donaldson made the highest break of the tournament scoring 115 during his semi-final match against John Pulman.

WIMBLEDON

Photo 1: Ted Schroeder receives the Men's Singles Trophy from the Duchess of Kent.
Photo 2: Margaret du Pont (left) and Louise Brough collect the Women's Doubles Trophy.

Men's Singles Champion - Ted Schroeder - United States
Ladies Singles Champion - Louise Brough - United States

The 1949 Wimbledon Championships took place on the outdoor grass courts at the All England Lawn Tennis and Croquet Club in Wimbledon, London, and ran from the 20th June until the 1st July. It was the 63rd staging of the Wimbledon Championships and the third Grand Slam tennis event of 1949.

Men's Singles Final:

Country	Player	Set 1	Set 2	Set 3	Set 4	Set 5
United States	Ted Schroeder	3	6	6	4	6
Czechoslovakia	Jaroslav Drobný	6	0	3	6	4

Women's Singles Final:

Country	Player	Set 1	Set 2	Set 3
United States	Louise Brough	10	1	10
United States	Margaret duPont	8	6	8

Men's Doubles Final:

Country	Players	Set 1	Set 2	Set 3
United States	Pancho Gonzales / Frank Parker	6	6	6
United States	Gardnar Mulloy / Ted Schroeder	4	4	2

Women's Doubles Final:

Country	Players	Set 1	Set 2
United States	Louise Brough / Margaret duPont	8	7
United States	Gussie Moran / Pat Todd	6	5

Mixed Doubles Final:

Country	Players	Set 1	Set 2	Set 3
South Africa	Eric Sturgess / Sheila Summers	9	9	7
Australia / United States	John Bromwich / Louise Brough	7	11	5

COUNTY CHAMPIONSHIP CRICKET WINNERS

Middlesex   **Yorkshire**

1949 saw the 50th officially organised running of the County Championship. The Championship was shared for the first time in its history between Middlesex County Cricket Club and Yorkshire County Cricket Club.

Pos.	Team	Pld.	W	L	D	Pts.
1	**Middlesex**	**26**	**14**	**3**	**9**	**192**
1	**Yorkshire**	**26**	**14**	**2**	**10**	**192**
3	Worcestershire	26	12	7	7	172
4	Warwickshire	26	12	5	8	168
5	Surrey	26	11	8	6	156

ENGLAND VS NEW ZEALAND - TEST SERIES

The New Zealand cricket team that toured England during the 1949 season was the fourth official touring side from New Zealand, following those in 1927, 1931 and 1937. The four-match Test series was shared, with every 3 day game ending in a draw.

1st Test | Headingley, Leeds, June 11th, 13th, 14th - Result: Match Drawn

Innings	Team	Score	Overs	Team	Score	Overs
1st Innings	England	372	127.3	New Zealand	341	118.3
2nd Innings	England	267/4d	68	New Zealand	195/2	49

2nd Test | Lord's, London, June 25th, 27th, 28th - Result: Match Drawn

Innings	Team	Score	Overs	Team	Score	Overs
1st Innings	England	313/9d	103.1	New Zealand	484	159.4
2nd Innings	England	306/5	68	New Zealand		

3rd Test | Old Trafford, Manchester, July 23rd, 25th, 26th - Result: Match Drawn

Innings	Team	Score	Overs	Team	Score	Overs
1st Innings	New Zealand	293	128.2	England	440/9d	128
2nd Innings	New Zealand	348/7	110	England		

4th Test | The Oval, London - August 13th, 15th, 16th - Result: Match Drawn

Innings	Team	Score	Overs	Team	Score	Overs
1st Innings	New Zealand	345	112.1	England	482	117.2
2nd Innings	New Zealand	308/9	97	England		

THE COST OF LIVING

COMPARISON CHART

	1949 Price	1949 Price Today (Including Inflation)	2018 Price	Real Term % Change
3 Bedroom House	£2,350	£81,267	£227,874	+180.4%
Weekly Income	£4.12s.2d	£159.36	£535	+235.7%
Pint Of Beer	10d	£1.44	£3.60	+150.0%
Cheese (lb)	2s.1d	£3.60	£3.38	-6.1%
Bacon (lb)	2s.2d	£3.75	£3.34	-10.9%
The Beano	2d	29p	£2.50	+762.1%

Cadburys Bourn-Vita Goodnight Drink (½lb)	1s.10½d
Nestlé's Milo Bedtime Drink (1lb)	4s
Rowntree's Fruit Gums	2½d
Brylcreem (jar)	1s.11½d
Wilkinson Razor	12s.10d
Amami Shampoo	4d
Arrid Cream Deodorant (jar)	2s.5d
Grossmith Face Powder	3s.9d
Pears Talcum Powder (tin)	1s.9d
Lux Toilet Soap (large bar)	10d
Astral Cream Soap (large bar)	8½d
Gibbs S.R. Toothpaste	1s.4d
Solidox Toothpaste	1s.1d
Toni Plastic Curlers	12s.6d
Prestoband Anti-Septic Self-Adhesive Bandages	5d
Cherry Blossom Boot Polish (large tin)	7d
Black & White Scotch Whisky	£1.13s.4d
Whiteway's Pale British Sherry	9s.6d
Hall's Wine	16s
Astorias Cigarettes (20)	3s.6d

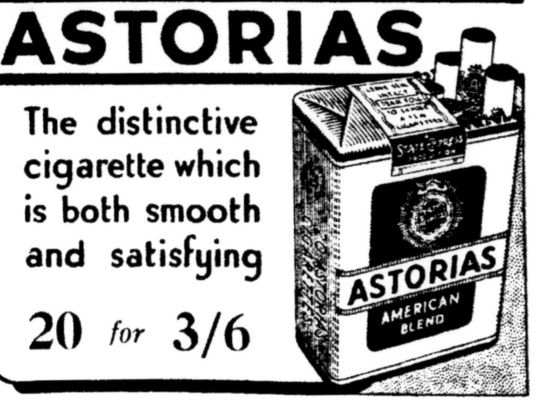

EVERYONE ENJOYS

ASTORIAS

The distinctive cigarette which is both smooth and satisfying

20 for 3/6

ASTORIAS AMERICAN BLEND

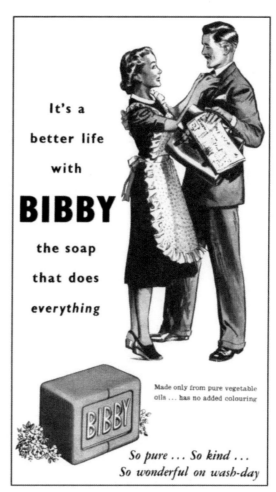

CLOTHES

Women's Clothing

Sodens Beaver Lamb Fur Coat	23 gns
Fenwicks Navy Town Coat	£6.5s
Pettits Jersey Wool Jacket	£1.10s.4d
Fenwicks Ballet Dance Dress	£3.18s.6d
Barkers Floral Afternoon Dress	£3.7s.10d
Barkers Woollen Mixture Cloth Skirt	£1.7s.2d
Thomas Wallis Crepe Pyjamas	£1.19s.11d
Jaeger Nightdress	£4.5s.6d
Barkers Swim Suit	15s
Satin Locknit Princess Slip	13s.11d
Thomas Wallis Roll-On Pantee	16s.9d
K-Shoes Roella Velvet Black Suede Shoes	£2.3s.9d
Jaeger Lady's Slippers	£1.1s.1d

Here comes the winner...

Here's the best looking — best behaving swimsuit we've ever made. It's specially for you if you want to swim better, look lovelier and have a heavenly time this summer. It's woven in dream coloured cotton-rayon-lastex material that takes years off a girl's figure—it's fast drying—stretches two ways and fits just like your own skin. Men too, can cut a dash in these ribbed for slimness, quick drying wool trunks. Plenty of people are waiting for the new Jantzens. So buy yours soon and have a happy holiday.

Jantzen makes swimmers slimmer

Eye-catching!

STEADFAST COLOUR FOR LOVELY LIPS!

Soft and glamorous . . . as a warm, perfumed night, when
the moon is a silver streak across the water; lasting and lustrous . . .
as pearls spilled upon a Tropic strand; flaring and flaunting . . .
as colours of the hibiscus. Yes . . that's Tattoo Lipstick . . .
daring . . . . . and oh so magical! With Tattoo's own secret
of indelibility! You just put it on . . let it set . . .
wipe it off . . . . . only the glowing colour remains!

CHOOSE FROM THIS GLORIOUS
RANGE OF *South Seas* SHADES!

1.	Tahiti Pink	8.	Dusky Lagoon
2.	Hula Pink	9.	Pago Red
3.	Tropic Dawn	10.	Black Magic
4.	Scarlet Lelani	11.	Grass Skirt
5.	Exotic Orchid	12.	Sultry Sun
6.	Passion Flower	13.	Hawaiian Fire
7.	Black Hibiscus	14.	Coral Sea

LARGE SIZE 7/6d.
(incl. 3/- tax)
Refills 4/2d. (incl. tax)
MEDIUM SIZE 3/4d.
(incl. 1/4d. tax)
Refills 2/6d. (incl. tax)
SMALL SIZE 1/8d.
(incl. 8d. tax)
Refills 11½d. (incl. tax)

TATTOO *tropical colours*

CLOTHES

Men's Clothing

Govt. Surplus Waterproof Oilskin Coat	7s.6d
Jaeger Scarf	12s.11d
Medium Size Cardigan	£2.16s.9d
Pontings Navy Blue Melton Trousers	£1.4s.3d
Jaeger Dressing Gown	14 gns
Slippers	£1.11s.11d

OTHER PRICES

Triumph 1800 Town & Country Saloon Car	£1425
Ford Anglia E494A Car	£309
BOAC Flight London To Sydney - Single (4½ days)	£260
Hercules Ex-Govt. Stock Cycles	£3.10s
Gamage De Luxe Cycle Dynamo Lighting Set	18s.6d
Qualcast Roller Lawn Mower	£7.8s.5d
AGA Mobel B Cooker	£85 to £115
Kingswood Walnut 3 Piece Bedroom Suite	£70.6s.6d
Selfridges Divan With Spring Interior Mattress (4ft)	£16.10s.8d
Barkers Cabinet Wringing Machine	£8.17s.6d
Civil Service Stores Deck Chair	£1.5s.8d
H. Samuel 3-Stone Platinum Set Diamond Engagement Ring	£14
H. Samuel 22ct. Gold Wedding Ring	£4
Barkers Electric Vacuum Cleaner	£71.13s.6d
Seymour 5-Valve 4-Wave AC/DC Radio	12½ gns
Oscillating Electric Fan	£4.15s
Portable Electric Paint Sprayer	7 gns
Combined Infra-Red & Radiant Heat Lamp	£3.9s.6d
Coffee-Master Percolator	£1.5s
Gamages High-Grade Binoculars	£6.2s.6d
Biro Deluxe Pen	£5.15s
Eatons 12in Teddy Bear	£1.3s.6
Leslie Marshall Sleeping Doll	19s.8d

MONEY CONVERSION TABLE

Old Money		Equivalent Today
Farthing	¼d	0.1p
Half Penny	½d	0.21p
Penny	1d	0.42p
Threepence	3d	1.25p
Sixpence	6d	2.5p
Shilling	1s	5p
Florin	2s	10p
Half Crown	2s.6d	12.5p
Crown	5s	25p
Ten Shillings	10s	50p
Pound	20s	£1
Guinea	21s	£1.05

"...Top Mechanical Quality"*

"**B**RIEFLY this thoroughly satisfying car of the highest quality does everything with a silky smoothness, a soothing quietness, and also in about the highest degree of riding comfort in front and back seats yet known, and with a precision and lightness of control which makes a driver feel on top of his form and which renders every mile a delight whether in town or out on the open road ... Throughout, there is that suggestion of top mechanical quality, exclusive to a tiny fraction of cars, which eludes detailed description."

★ *A short extract from the Road Test Report on the Rover 75 published in The Autocar for February 4th, 1949.*

VISITORS TO BRITAIN Buy a Rover for use during *your stay and for subsequent export. Overseas dealers have arranged with the Company to give early delivery in this country from their export quota. Write us for particulars.*

ROVER

One of Britain's Fine Cars

THE ROVER COMPANY LIMITED, SOLIHULL, BIRMINGHAM AND DEVONSHIRE HOUSE, LONDON

Printed in Great
Britain
by Amazon